PEOPLE & PLACES

U.S.A.

Written by

Martha Ellen Zenfell

Consultant Kenneth S. Cooper

Illustrated by

Ann Savage

M

MACMILLAN

A TEMPLAR BOOK

First published in Great Britain in 1988
by Macmillan Children's Books
A division of Macmillan Publishers Ltd
4 Little Essex Street
London WC2R 3LF and Basingstoke

Devised and produced by Templar Publishing Ltd
107 High Street, Dorking, Surrey RH4 1QA

Editor Steve Parker
Designers Patrick Nugent, Bridget Morley
Photo-researcher Hugh Olliff
Studio services Kenneth Ward

Colour separations by Positive Colour Ltd, Maldon, Essex
Printed by L.E.G.O., Vicenza, Italy

British Library Cataloguing in Publication Data
Zenfell, Martha Ellen
    USA.—(People and places).
    1. United States—For children
    I. Title   II. Savage, Ann, 1951-
    III. Series
    973.927

ISBN 0 333 46605 5

Contents

WHERE IN THE WORLD?

The United States of America (USA) is the fourth-largest country in the world, after the USSR, Canada and China. It extends for almost 5,000 kilometres from the Atlantic Ocean on the east coast, to the Pacific on the west, and 3,000 kilometres from Canada in the north to Mexico in the south. There are two other, separate parts of the USA. These are the islands that make up the state of Hawaii, in the Pacific Ocean 3,360 kilometres west of California; and the state of Alaska, which is north-west of Canada.

The USA is so vast that from west to east it spans four different time zones. When it is four o'clock in the afternoon in New York, on the east coast, it is only one o'clock in Los Angeles, on the west coast. The USA's population is unevenly distributed across the country. Nearly three-quarters of Americans live in cities. Some states are densely populated while others are mostly deserts and barren lands, with very few people.

The USA is one of the world's richest countries. It has vast natural resources and enormous agricultural and industrial output. Because of its wealth, military might and popular culture (page 38) its influence reaches to the far corners of the globe.

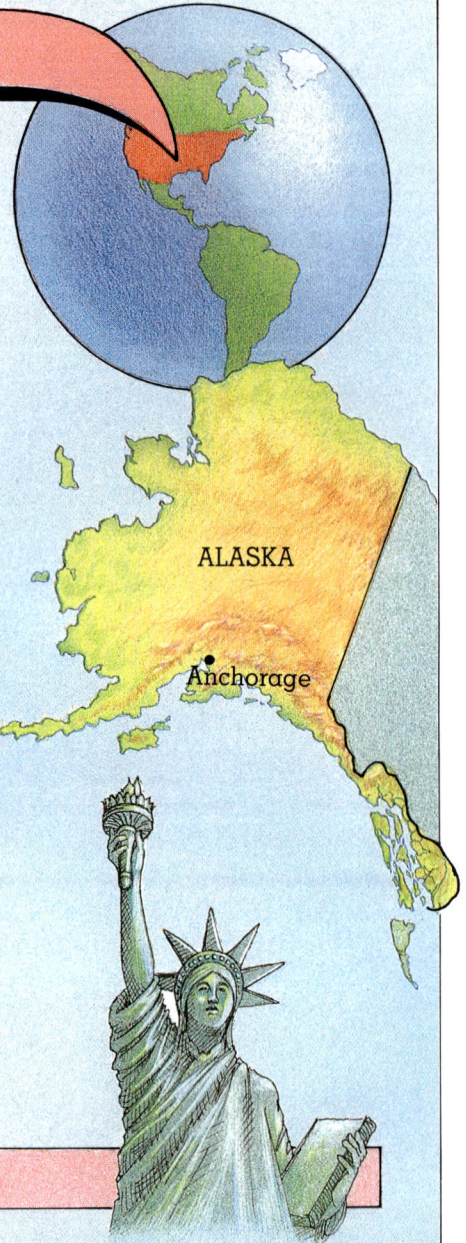

ALASKA

Anchorage

Symbols of the USA

The American flag is also known as the "Stars and Stripes". Red stands for courage, blue for justice and white for liberty. The 13 stripes represent the original colonies created by the early European settlers. The 50 stars stand for the 50 states of today. Millions of Americans are descended from Europeans who settled in America around the turn of this century. For them the Statue of Liberty, in New York harbour was a symbol of "The Land of the Free".

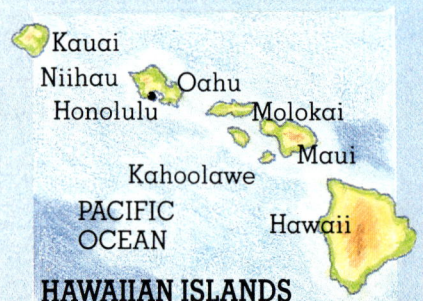

Kauai
Niihau
Honolulu
Oahu
Molokai
Maui
Kahoolawe
PACIFIC
OCEAN
Hawaii

HAWAIIAN ISLANDS

6

▶ The USA has a land area of 9,363,128 square kilometres (one million square kilometres less than the area of Europe).

▶ The population is 250 million people.

▶ There are 50 states, each with its own state capital.

▶ The national capital of the USA is Washington, in the tiny territory of District of Columbia (often called Washington, DC).

▶ This territory was created specially so that the national capital would not "belong" to any one state.

▶ The unit of currency is the US *dollar*, which is divided into 100 *cents*.

▶ The official language is English.

▶ The religion with most followers is Christianity. There is no official state religion, and many people follow other faiths such as Judaism.

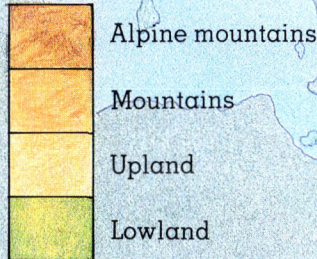

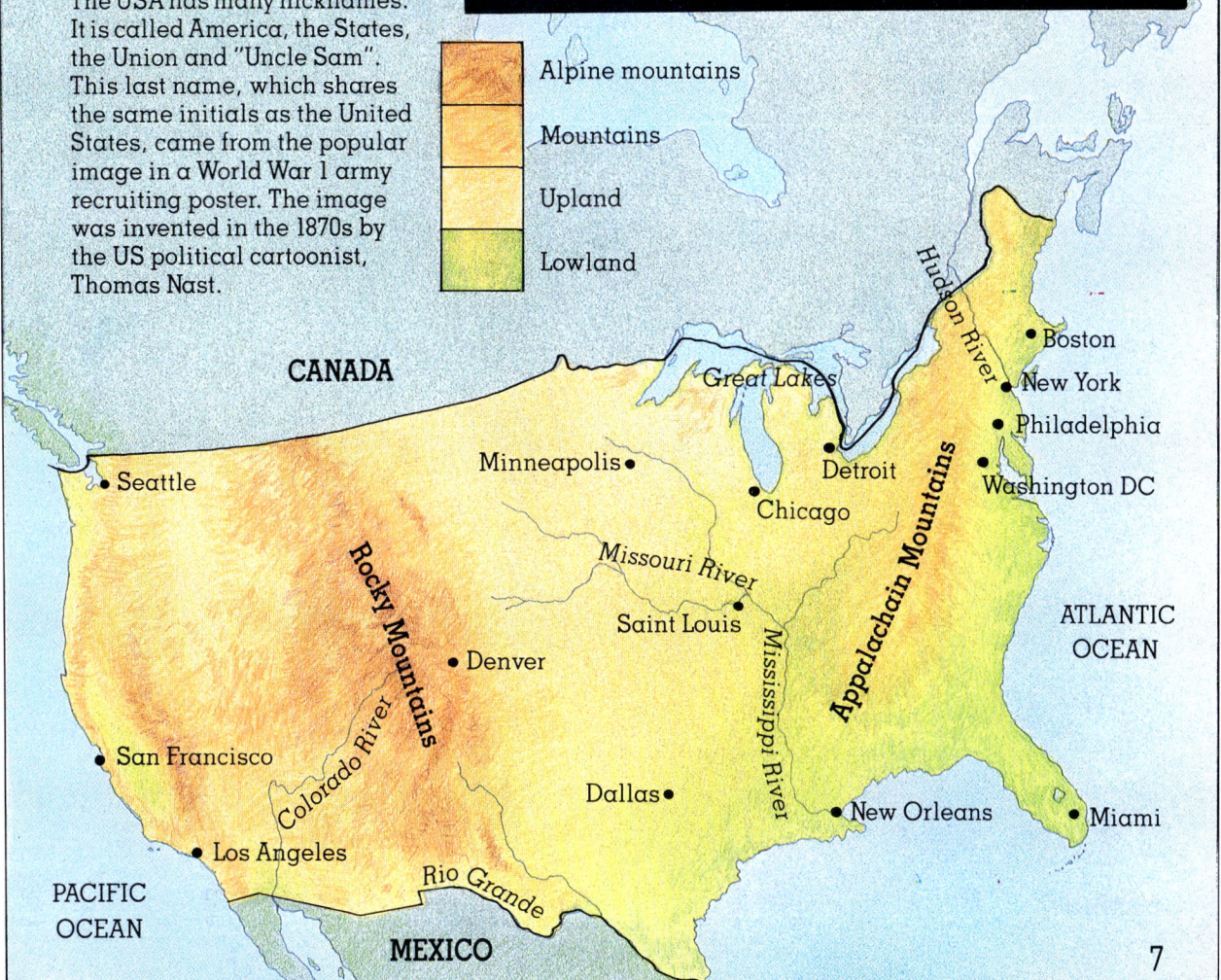

"Uncle Sam"

The USA has many nicknames. It is called America, the States, the Union and "Uncle Sam". This last name, which shares the same initials as the United States, came from the popular image in a World War 1 army recruiting poster. The image was invented in the 1870s by the US political cartoonist, Thomas Nast.

Alpine mountains

Mountains

Upland

Lowland

CANADA

Seattle

Minneapolis

Great Lakes

Detroit

Hudson River

Boston

New York

Philadelphia

Washington DC

Rocky Mountains

Missouri River

Saint Louis

Appalachain Mountains

ATLANTIC OCEAN

Chicago

Denver

Colorado River

Mississippi River

San Francisco

Dallas

Los Angeles

New Orleans

Miami

Rio Grande

PACIFIC OCEAN

MEXICO

MOUNTAINS, DESERTS AND PLAINS

The landscape of the USA varies enormously. Within its borders are deserts, snow-capped mountains, fertile farmlands and semi-tropical rainforests.

Most of the southern states have hot summers and cool or cold winters. The northern states tend to have a brief warm summer and a long cold winter. Alaska, in the far north-west, is almost always cold because it is on the Arctic Circle.

In the south are enormous areas of lowland farming land. In the north are wheat-covered plains and the picturesque Great Lakes. The Appalachian Mountains, in the east, are of poor agricultural quality, but rich in coal and iron ore. In the south-west lie deserts and shrublands. Towering above them are the Rocky Mountains (often called the Rockies), running north-south, which rise to over 4,000 metres. The Great Basin lies between the state of California, on the west coast, and the Rockies. It is a rock-strewn desert, almost completely uninhabited.

The middle of the USA, known as the Midwest, is the "breadbasket" of America. Here, thousands of square kilometres of corn (Indian corn or maize) and wheat are grown.

The island state

The 130 islands of the state of Hawaii are warm and tropical. Hawaii is the USA's newest state, joining the country in 1959. The capital of Hawaii is Honolulu, on the island of Oahu. Hawaii's beautiful beaches such as Waikiki Beach (below), fringed with palm trees, make it a favourite holiday resort with Americans and other visitors.

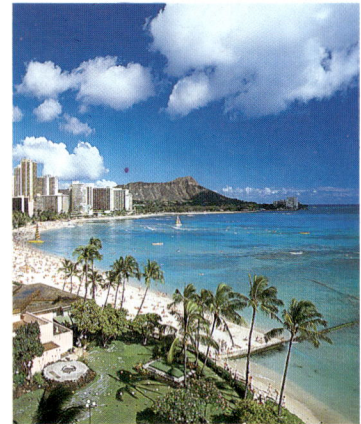

The northernmost state

Alaska borders the Arctic and North Pacific Oceans. It is the biggest US state, and one of the least populated, with only half a million people in its 1,530,693 square kilometres. A land of glaciers, lakes and marshes, peopled mainly by Inuit (Eskimos), it lies so far north there are less than four hours of sunlight each day during winter. The highest point on the continent of North America, Mount McKinley, (6,194 metres), is located in central Alaska.

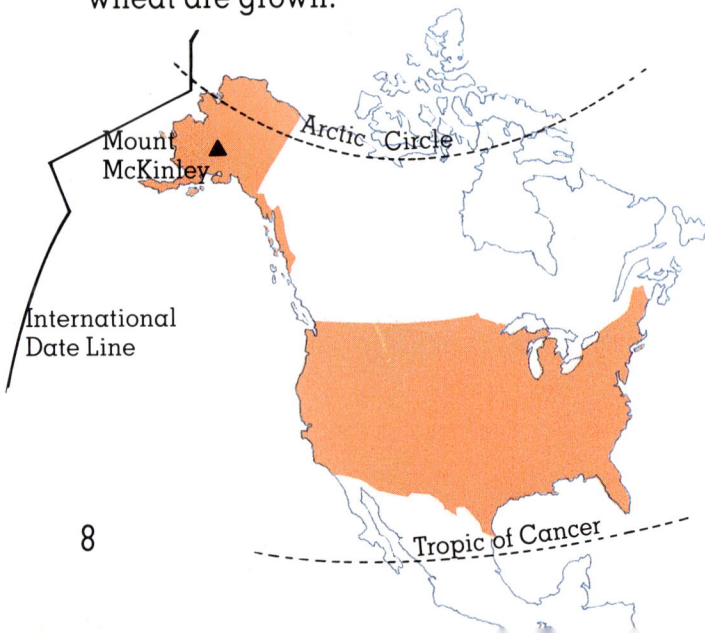

The Grand Canyon

The Colorado Plateau, in the south-west of the USA, covers about 330,000 square kilometres. Rivers flowing across the plateau have cut huge canyons into the rock. The most spectacular is the Grand Canyon, 350 kilometres long and between 6 and 29 kilometres wide. In places its cliff-like walls tower 1,500 metres above the Colorado River below.

"Old Man River"

The mighty Mississippi River runs from north to south through the heartland of the USA. It drains a huge area, from the Appalachian Mountains in the east to the Rocky Mountains in the west. Historically it was an important commercial waterway, with paddlesteamers such as this one carrying passengers and goods. The Mississippi has a large tributary, the Missouri. Together, they form the fourth longest river in the world (at 6,020 kilometres).

THE WILD LANDS

Much of the USA is still relatively wild, where animals roam freely and vegetation is left to flourish. These lands are protected by the US government, and are called National Parks. In the National Parks there is no felling of trees, no grazing of livestock, no digging for minerals, and no hunting of wild animals, except for reasons of conservation.

The scenery of National Parks ranges from the snow-capped mountains of the west to the cypress-lined swamps of the south-east, in the state of Florida. The parks are popular for camping and walking holidays. They are safe havens for famous animals and trees native to the USA, such as bristlecone pines (the world's oldest trees), pumas (also called cougars or mountain lions), grizzly bears and buffaloes.

The nation's largest wildlife sanctuary is Yellowstone Park, in the north-west. It is also one of the oldest National Parks. Wolves, coyotes, antelopes, elks and buffaloes roam at will through Yellowstone's 8,982 square kilometres. Two of the country's rarest species also live here: the bald eagle (America's national bird), and the grizzly bear.

Yellowstone also has hot water springs (geysers). The best known is "Old Faithful", which erupts about once every hour, spurting out 35,000 litres of hot water 45 metres into the air.

The call of the coyote
A dweller on the North American plains is the coyote (pronounced "kie-owe-tee"). Also called a prairie wolf, it hunts alone or in packs and eats food ranging from insects to small deer. Coyotes communicate by mournful-sounding howls.

Opossums
The rat-like opossum is one of the few marsupials found outside Australia. Sometimes called the "possum", it is active at night and eats fruit and small creatures. It ranges from Mexico through the USA into Canada.

Sequoia National Park

The world's largest trees, in terms of weight, are giant sequoias (redwoods, shown on the left). They grow in Sequoia National Park, in central California. One tree, called the General Sherman, is at least 3,500 years old, 83 metres tall, and 11 metres in diameter. The world's tallest trees, the coastal redwoods, flourish nearby in northern California. Some specimens grow to more than 110 metres high.

Buffaloes in danger

The buffalo (bison) is native to the North American continent. A century ago, many large herds roamed the plains. Hunted by both the North American Indians and American settlers, the population dwindled from almost 75 million to just 1,000 animals. Today, due to strict conservation, there are about 10,000 buffaloes in the USA.

WHEAT FOR THE WORLD

American farmers are the world leaders in agricultural produce. Exports on a large scale include corn (maize), citrus fruits, meat, milk, tobacco and wheat. Food accounts for approximately one-fifth of the value of all US exports. Eating imported foreign food, like French cheeses, is considered a luxury in many areas. However, imported grapes, bananas and other fruits are becoming more common in shops in winter.

There are distinct farming regions within the USA. Dairy products come mainly from the north, around the Great Lakes region. The Midwest is known as the "Corn Belt", where corn (maize) is grown. Wheat is grown in different parts of the USA at different times of the year. Special strains of wheat grow in the cold winters of the Midwest; in summer, it is sown farther north.

The south used to be known as the "Cotton Belt". Nowadays, much of this flat, damp land has been flooded and fields of rice have taken the place of billowing fields of fluffy white-headed cotton plants.

California and Florida harvest lush, tropical fruits like oranges, lemons and avocados. Tobacco, which is exported all over the world, comes from states on the Atlantic Coast, such as Virginia and North Carolina.

Round-up time
Much farming in the USA is now done by large machines. However, the cowboy still plays an all-important role. Working on horseback is still an efficient way of moving huge herds of cattle from one area to another. Kansas City, the largest town in the Midwest, established its reputation through cattle and meat markets (and jazz bands).

"Amber waves of grain"
The famous US song *America the Beautiful* begins: "Oh beautiful for spacious skies and amber waves of grain..." This refers to the endless wheat fields of the Midwest and North-west. The USA is the world's second-largest producer of wheat (after the USSR) and the leading exporter.

Slaves to cotton
In the 1700s, people were brought from Africa to work as slaves on the cotton fields of the south. They were kept as virtual prisoners and forced to work long hours for meagre food. In 1865 slavery was abolished in the USA (see page 28). This picture of 1884 shows a cotton plantation near the Mississippi.

MINERAL WEALTH GALORE

The USA is enormously rich in natural resources. The country extracts, refines and exports large quantities of petroleum, copper, fertilizer materials and coal. Coal and petroleum are important energy resources at home. In recent years, regions with many hours of sunlight, like California, have been experimenting with solar power as a source of energy.

The USA is both the largest oil consumer and one of the biggest producers of natural gas and oil (petroleum) – although the Middle East has bigger reserves. The cost of extracting petroleum on most American fields is much higher than in the Middle East, due partly to the higher wages of the workers.

More than four-fifths of the country's petroleum output is converted into gasoline (petrol), diesel and other motor fuels and oils. With the USA's dependence on the automobile, offshore drilling is now commonplace in California and the Gulf of Mexico, as the original oil fields of Texas run dry.

Instant millionaires

Some Texan cattle farmers discovered petroleum (oil) on their ranches, making them millionaires practically overnight. The first Texan oil well, called Spindletop, was discovered in 1901. Oil fields were then found in many parts of the state, over the next few decades. Pumps to raise the oil, called "nodding donkeys" (above), are still seen in many areas.

The "Diggers of '49"

Today, little remains of the gold which brought "diggers" to California from all parts of the USA, in the gold rush of 1848-49. The chance of finding this most precious of minerals opened up the western part of the USA. In 1848, California's population was about 14,000. By 1860 it was 380,000. Here, mine workers sift rocks and sand for gold flakes, in 1852.

Bingham copper mine

Copper, used for making
electrical wire, is mined in
great quantities in the USA's
south-west. This copper mine
at Bingham Canyon, Utah, is
one of the world's largest.
Arizona is the leading copper-
producing state in the USA.

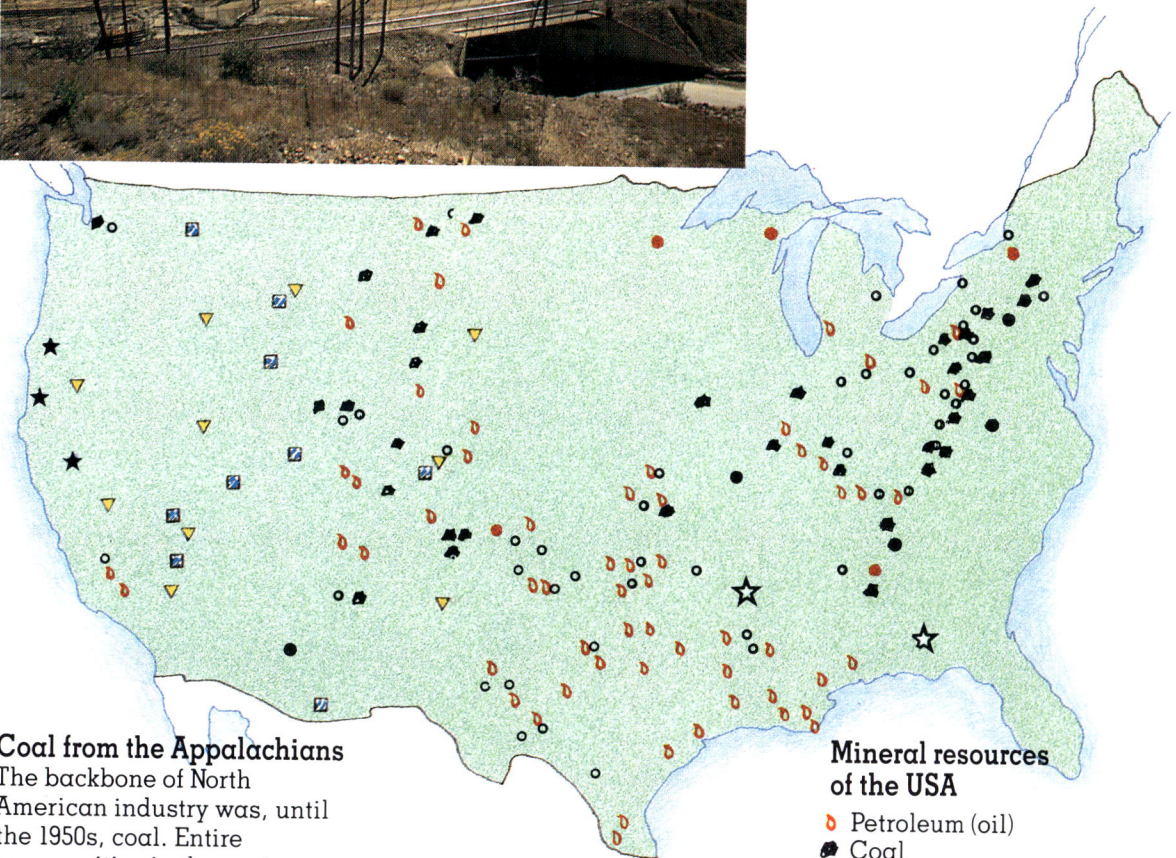

Coal from the Appalachians

The backbone of North
American industry was, until
the 1950s, coal. Entire
communities in the eastern
part of the country, especially
along the Appalachian
Mountains, sprang up to mine
this valuable mineral. Modern
mining techniques and the
discovery of other resources
(shown on the map) has
meant the closure of many coal
mines.

Mineral resources of the USA

- ⏺ Petroleum (oil)
- ⬤ Coal
- ○ Natural gas
- ● Iron ore
- ▽ Bauxite (aluminium ore)
- ▧ Gold
- ★ Silver
- ☆ Chromium

15

STEELYARDS AND SPACE SHUTTLES

Heavy industry, such as car production, depends on steel. Steel is made from iron ore, which was plentiful in the USA. However, many of the steel mills on the USA's east coast now use ore imported from South America, because US supplies are running low. The USA now imports one-third of the ore it needs to make steel.

Towns such as Milwaukee and Chicago, on the Great Lakes, flourished because of the steel industry. These cities are now undergoing change, as the USA's heavy industry becomes less competitive compared to Far Eastern production. Nuclear power, once thought to be an inexpensive energy source, has become a controversial issue because of possible radioactive pollution. Nuclear power stations along waterways like the Mississippi River and the Great Lakes have been the site of public protests.

The American car industry, which began in the 1900s, has, until recently, been very successful. An American, Henry Ford, was responsible for making automobiles cheap enough to be bought by ordinary people. Between 1908 and 1914 he standardised the manufacture of car parts and introduced assembly-line production to manufacture the Model T Ford car. It was cheap compared with its rivals, and enabled millions of Americans to own a motor vehicle. The USA's car industry reached peak production in the 1950s and 60s when Detroit, on Lake Erie, earned the nickname "Motor City". In the 1970s the world price of petroleum, and therefore of the gasoline (petrol) made from it, rose sharply. The large-engined American cars became expensive to run. Also, people questioned the wisdom of using up precious resources of petroleum so fast, and polluting the air with exhaust fumes.

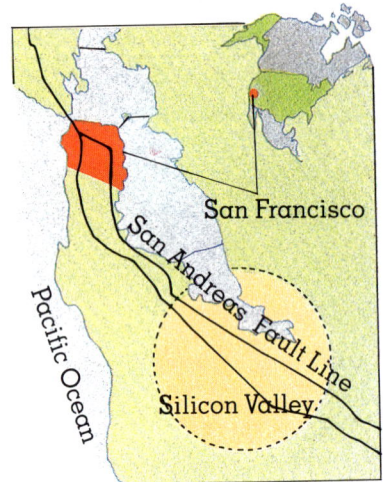

Silicon Valley

The development of the electronic computer has meant boomtime for a former fruit-growing area in northern California. It is now known as Silicon Valley, one of the high-tech capitals of the world. Some of the world's most advanced computers and programs have been produced here.

The "Dream Machine"

During the late 1950s and early 1960s, the US car producers were making large and lavish chrome-decorated models such as the 1957 Ford Edsel on the right. Owning such a car became a symbol of wealth and national pride. However, these cars were enormously costly to fuel and maintain. Today, they are mostly collectors' items.

"A giant leap for mankind"

In 1961 US President John Kennedy set a goal to put a man on the Moon by the end of the decade. NASA (National Aeronautics and Space Administration) was set up. On 21 July 1969, Neil Armstrong spoke these words as he became the first man on the Moon: "That's one small step for a man, one giant leap for mankind". The project cost $24 billion. The current US space programme relies on the Space Shuttle, a rocket-plane that can make many trips into space. (Before the Shuttle, each rocket could be used only once.) However, the programme was put back by the explosion of a Shuttle in January 1986, which killed all seven crew members. Many Americans lost confidence in the programme and wanted the money to be spent on tackling poverty, pollution and other more down-to-earth problems.

AMERICANS ON THE MOVE

mericans always seem to be on the move. Many young people have their own car at 16, and a popular family holiday is to "get in the car and discover America". This is made possible through a huge network of roads, from dusty country tracks to 10-lane freeways (motorways).

North America was the first continent to create a system of roads designed specifically for the motor car. The national government pays for some roads and individual states pay for others, sometimes charging drivers a toll (fee) to drive on them. Toll roads are often called "turnpikes".

The USA is so vast that domestic airline travel has undergone a boom in the last 20 years. Tickets are inexpensive enough for people to fly from city to city, rather than drive. Busy airports like O'Hare in Chicago have several hundred domestic flights a day, serving all of the USA, as well as international flights. Several US airlines fly internationally, such as TWA, Pan Am and Delta.

The Amtrak train
This is one of the few passenger-carrying trains left in the USA. Most trains today carry only freight. Railways, which were an important mode of transport in the 19th century, have given way to cars and planes. Many Americans today have never been on a train.

The Greyhound bus
The Greyhound company operates a nationwide system of coaches that offer inexpensive travel. Greyhounds are often used by tourists who want to see the countryside, without spending too many dollars.

The first aeroplane flight
The brothers Orville and Wilbur Wright made the first successful powered aeroplane flight at Kitty Hawk, North Carolina, in 1903 (shown above). By 1906 they were able to stay airborne for more than an hour. Nowadays, there are more than 16,000 licensed airports and airfields in the USA. Catching a plane, for many Americans, is like taking a coach or train for Europeans.

Spaghetti junctions
There are more than 100 million cars in the USA today. In Los Angeles, it is not uncommon for people to drive 150 kilometres to work and back each day. This tangle of flyovers and underpasses is in Seattle, near the west coast.

19

LAND OF THE SKYSCRAPER

America's cities embrace many architectural styles. There are Spanish and French influences in New Orleans, elegant colonial-style buildings in Washington DC and the high-tech, high-rise skyscrapers of New York. Philadelphia and Boston look rather like English cities, because they were founded by settlers from Britain in the 17th century.

In recent years, many people have moved to city suburbs, which has created new urban areas as skyscrapers have reached the countryside. It is sometimes difficult to tell where one city's suburbs end and another's begin!

Washington, DC

The nation's capital is one of the USA's few "planned" settlements, designed by a French military engineer. Rising out of marshland, it lies between the states of Maryland and Virginia. Avenues are broad, skyscrapers are few, and the nation's government buildings are surrounded by trees. Washington is an orderly, graceful city of some 650,000 inhabitants.

New York, New York

Most people's image of New York city is of the skyscraper-dominated island of Manhattan, only 20 kilometres long by 3 kilometres wide. Manhattan's towering skyline includes the World Trade Centre twin skyscrapers, the Empire State Building, the financial area of Wall Street, the theatres and cinemas of Broadway, the artistic quarter of Greenwich Village, and Central Park. In reality, New York City has several districts apart from Manhattan, such as Brooklyn, the Bronx and Queens. It is often called New York City (NYC), to distinguish it from New York State. It is the largest city in the USA, with eight million people.

Capitol Hill, Washington DC

Home of jazz

Few American cities can compete with the beauty of New Orleans. It was founded by the French and later became Spanish, and these influences can be seen in its architecture. Jazz music originated in the city in the late 19th century. Today, New Orleans preserves its heritage with care, as can be seen in its broad avenues, canopied buildings (as shown on the left), and jazz and blues bars. It is built on the banks of the Mississippi and is home to about 570,000 people.

The subtropical south

Miami's warm climate, even in the middle of winter, attracts many visitors. Tourism is one of its biggest industries (as is the growing of citrus fruits). Hotels and souvenir shops line its beaches, and swimsuits are not out of place even in its main streets. Miami has a population of about 350,000 and is the second largest city in Florida, after Jacksonville.

21

THE FIRST AMERICANS

No one knows for sure when the first inhabitants came to the USA, although it seems to have been around 20,000 years ago. When the European explorer Christopher Columbus sailed there in 1492 he named the inhabitants "Indians", because he thought he had sailed around the world to Asia and landed in India. The "Indians" were in fact many different groups of peoples, each with their own names and customs.

North American Indians were not the wild warriors we commonly see in old "Western" films. More cowboys died of the disease cholera than at the hands of the North American Indians. Most Indians were peaceable people who lived in harmony with nature, taking enough for food and shelter from the land, but not destroying it. Some of the main groups are shown on the map opposite.

The desert peoples

North American Indians of the south-west were desert people. They built shelters of mud and irrigated the dry land to grow fields of crops. They also made pottery and jewellery. Groups include the Apache, Navajo (on the right), Pueblo and Ute.

KEY FACTS

► When Columbus arrived in the "New World" in 1492, there were perhaps 10 million people living in the area we now call the USA.
► Diseases brought by European settlers, such as smallpox and measles, killed millions of North American Indians.
► More than 200 different languages were spoken in the area of present-day California, when the Europeans arrived.
► About 40 main groups of North American Indians lived on the Great Plains in the central USA and Canada.
► They hunted buffaloes and other animals on foot. Horses were only introduced by European settlers from about 1600.

Indian princess

Pocahontas, the daughter of Indian chief Powhatan, is thought to have saved the life of the English settler Captain John Smith in 1608. Pocahontas later married an Englishman, John Rolfe, and sailed to England. She was received as royalty at the court of King James I. Planning her return to the USA, she died of smallpox and was buried in the chancel of Gravesend church, England.

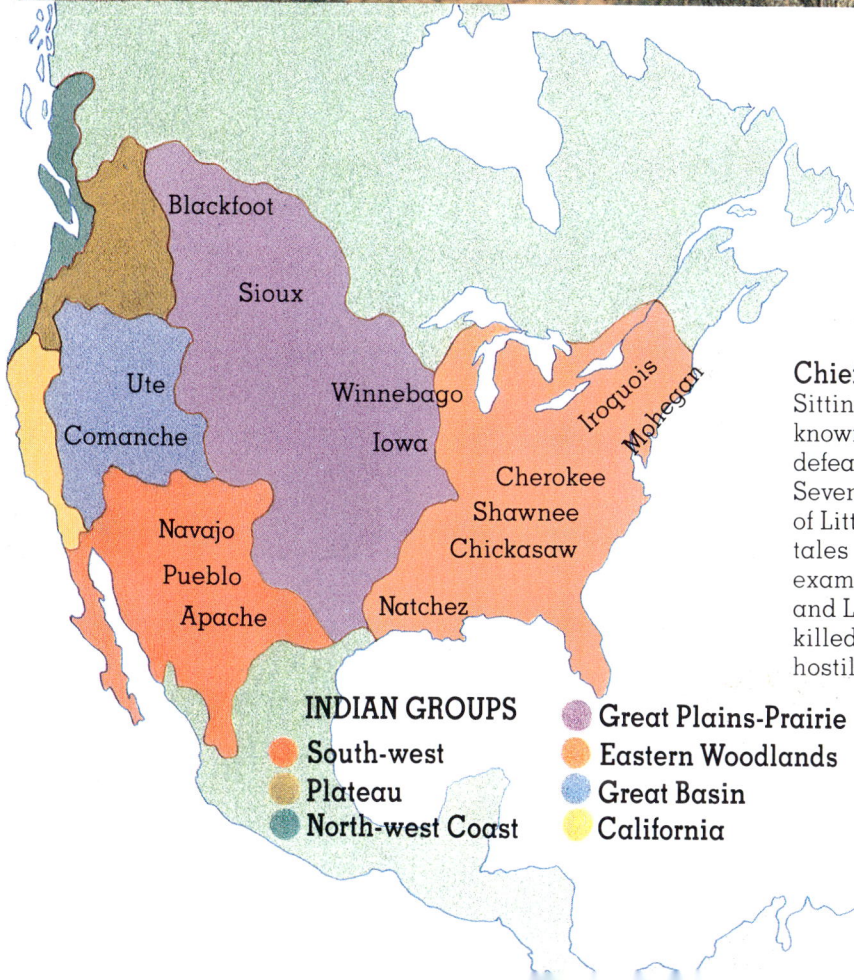

Chief Sitting Bull

Sitting Bull was a Sioux chief known mainly for his successful defeat of General Custer and the Seventh Cavalry in the Battle of Little Big Horn, 1876. Many tales were told about him, for example, that he wrote French and Latin poems. He was killed in 1890, during further hostilities.

Blackfoot

Sioux

Ute

Comanche

Winnebago

Iowa

Iroquois

Mohegan

Cherokee

Shawnee

Chickasaw

Navajo

Pueblo

Apache

Natchez

INDIAN GROUPS

- South-west
- Plateau
- North-west Coast
- Great Plains-Prairie
- Eastern Woodlands
- Great Basin
- California

THE "NEW WORLD"

The continents of North and South America were named after Amerigo Vespucci, an Italian explorer, in around 1507. Viking explorers had landed in north-east North America in the 10th and 11th centuries. But the great wave of European exploration and colonization was begun by Christopher Columbus, who landed in the "New World" in 1492.

America's early settlers were mainly from Britain. Some came to escape religious persecution, others to establish a new way of life. The first permanent colony, Jamestown, was set up in Virginia in 1609.

By the mid-1700s, 13 colonies had been established along the eastern coast by European settlers. Each colony had an independent government but was under the overall control of Britain. Colonists named these new settlements after their original countries and towns: New England, New Amsterdam, New Sweden, New York and New Jersey.

The independent spirit, and strong feelings of new nationalism, led to resentment among the colonists about paying taxes to Britain. This grew into a rebellion and in 1775 the American Revolution (American War of Independence) began against the British. A Declaration of Independence was signed by the Americans on 4 July, 1776. In 1781, after years of bloody fighting, the USA won. Two years later the USA's independence was recognized by Europe, at the signing of the Treaty of Paris.

The Quakers
In 1681 William Penn, a member of the Quaker religious group, received a charter from Britain to set up a colony he called Pennsylvania. Philadelphia, one of his towns, became the largest city in colonial America.

Thanksgiving Day

The North American Indians were often helpful to the early settlers, teaching them about the land and the crops which could be grown. After one particularly successful harvest, the grateful settlers gathered with the Indians for a feast, to give thanks for their stores of food that would last through the harsh winter. This was the first Thanksgiving Day. This day is now celebrated all over the USA, on the third Thursday in November, with family feasts of traditional food including turkey and pumpkin pie.

Declaration of Independence

The Declaration of Independence in 1776 stated the rights of the USA as a free country, no longer under British colonial rule. This painting by John Trumbull shows the event. Americans now celebrate Independence Day with parties and fireworks, every 4 July.

Father of the Union

In 1789, 13 years after the USA became independent, George Washington became the first US president. He had been commander-in-chief of the army during the War of Independence against Britain. He was an able administrator and remained president until 1797. By the time of his death in 1799, the USA was a powerful and expanding nation.

OPENING UP AMERICA

During its first 100 years as an independent nation, the USA evolved from a land of mainly scattered rural settlements into a larger, thriving industrial country. The Louisiana Purchase (1803) doubled the size of the country overnight. President Thomas Jefferson arranged to buy land originally colonized by France, for about $15 million. The two million square kilometres of land purchased stretched westward from the Mississippi River to the Rocky Mountains.

In the Mexican War (1846-1848) Mexico and the USA fought over who owned land on the border between the two countries. When the USA won it gained vast new territories in the south-west. The discovery of gold in California, in 1848, took people westward, and pioneers braved the difficulties of living in these new lands that became known as the "Wild West". Many stories are told about the people who pushed westwards across the USA, settling the newly acquired territories. Jesse James (an outlaw), Wild Bill Hickok (marshall of Kansas), Buffalo Bill and Annie Oakley (a member of Buffalo Bill's Wild West Show) are famous names from the 19th century, when the six-shooter gun often had more effect than the rule of law.

However, many of the "cowboy" legends are exaggerated. Buffalo Bill Cody supposedly killed thousands of buffaloes and North American Indians single-handed. In fact, his nickname came from supplying buffalo meat to railroad workers. He did not kill buffaloes for sport and was against the killing of Indians. From 1869 he toured the USA, and later Europe, taking part in "Wild West" shows with performing rodeo riders, Indian hunters and staged buffalo hunts.

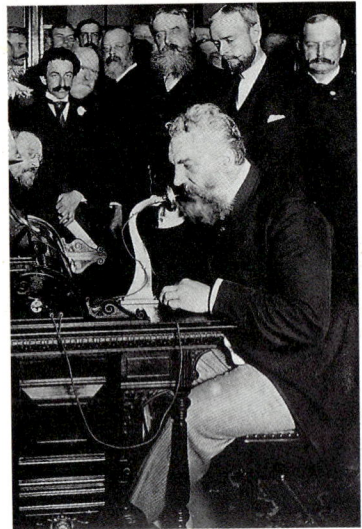

Land of invention
At the same time as the western areas were being opened up, the USA's economic growth continued in the east. Industry and agriculture thrived. The 19th century saw the invention of the telegraph and the phonograph (record player). Other US "firsts" include the steamboat, the electric light and, in the 1880s in Chicago, the building of the first skyscrapers. The telephone was also invented in the USA, by Alexander Bell (above). He was born in 1847 in Scotland but moved to the USA as a young man. In 1876 he made the first telephone. A recent survey shows that over half the 'phones in the world are owned by Americans.

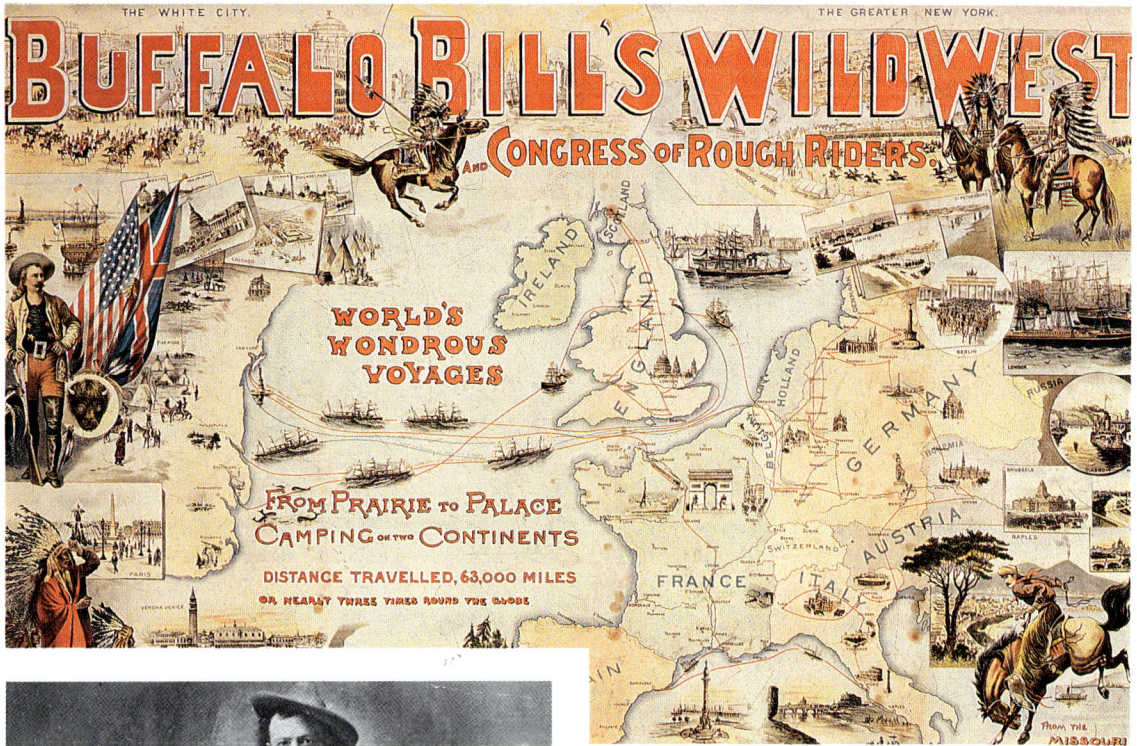

THE WHITE CITY.   THE GREATER NEW YORK.

BUFFALO BILL'S WILD WEST
AND CONGRESS OF ROUGH RIDERS.

WORLD'S
WONDROUS
VOYAGES

FROM PRAIRIE TO PALACE
CAMPING ON TWO CONTINENTS

DISTANCE TRAVELLED, 63,000 MILES
OR NEARLY THREE TIMES ROUND THE GLOBE

FROM THE
MISSOURI

Wild Bill   Texas Jack   Buffalo Bill

The "legend" of the Wild West

People in Europe, and even in the east of the USA, formed their ideas of the "Wild West" from rumours and tales of outlaws, gunfights and battles with Indians. Buffalo Bill's Wild West Show toured Europe, as the poster above shows, and helped to spread some of these legends. The reality was rather different, as shown by the photograph on the left. This depicts James "Wild Bill" Hickok, "Texas Jack" Omohundro, and William "Buffalo Bill" Cody (before his show began).

A NATION DIVIDED

One of the most tragic events in American history was the Civil War (1861-65), fought between the northern and southern states. The wealth of the southern states came from cotton and the south depended on the black slaves who picked and processed it. Many people in the northern states thought that slavery was cruel and unnecessary.

In 1861, the argument over slavery came to a head when northern politicians refused to allow slavery to spread into the newly settled western regions. Some angry southern states withdrew from the Union and set up their own country, the Confederate States of America. War followed and the two sides of the bitterly divided nation fought each other for four years. About 620,000 Americans were killed.

After the war some feelings of resentment and hatred continued and still influence American society today. Black Americans, some of whom are descended from freed slaves, continued to campaign for their rights as citizens in recent years.

The turning point

One of the major events in the American Civil War was the Battle of Gettysburg, in 1863. The Confederates were pushing northwards, hoping to replenish food and supplies from lands captured from the Union. But at Gettysburg, they were turned back by forces from the north. This photograph shows the town of Gettysburg and the soldiers' camp. After this victory for the north, Union troops under Generals Ulysses Grant and William Sherman fought their way south, inflicting enormous casualties on the other side. In April 1865, the Confederate forces, under their brilliant commander Robert Lee, were finally outnumbered, and surrendered to Grant at Appomattox Court House.

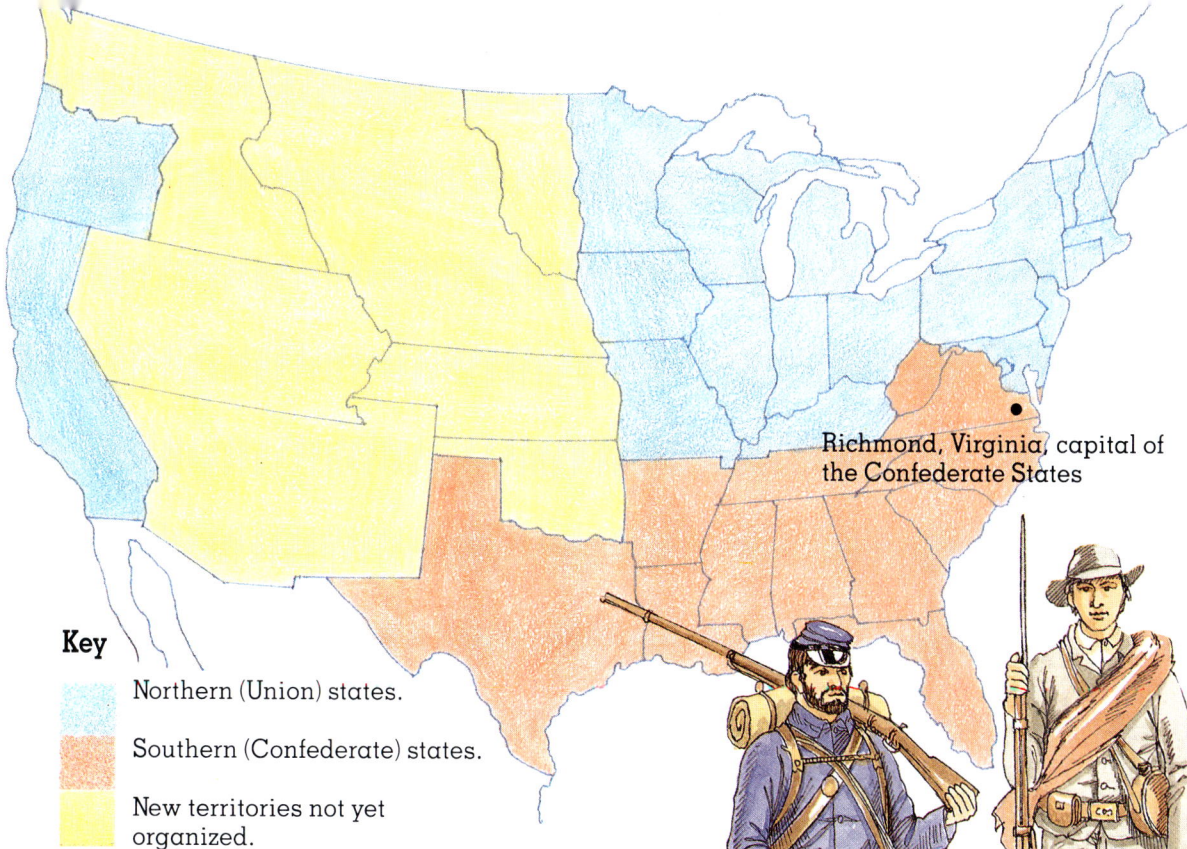

Richmond, Virginia, capital of the Confederate States

Key

Northern (Union) states.

Southern (Confederate) states.

New territories not yet organized.

North versus south

The map above shows which states were involved in the Civil War. The Union states represented about 22 million people, while some nine million people lived in the south. About three and a half million southerners were black, and saw their chance of freedom if the north won.

"Honest Abe"

Abraham Lincoln (1809-65) was President of the Union during the American Civil War. He was against slavery and oversaw its abolition in 1865. He is considered by many historians to be the greatest US president. He was shot dead by a supporter of the southern states while watching a play at Ford's Theatre, Washington, DC.

Confederate soldier

Union soldier

Civil War soldiers

Union soldiers, fighting for the north, were usually better equipped and organized than the south's Confederate army. Towards the end of the conflict the Confederate soldiers lacked guns, ammunition and food, and some even marched barefoot.

TIMES OF CHANGE

The 20th century has seen an enormous number of world events involving the USA. The country's attempts at flight have progressed from building the first powered aeroplane to putting a man on the Moon – in 66 years! The USA has built up its military might to become one of the two most powerful global forces (with the USSR).

The USA's population nearly doubled in the first half of the 20th century, from 76 million in 1900 to 151 million in 1950. Boatloads of people arrived in New York harbour from southern and eastern Europe and from Ireland, which is why so many Americans have Polish, Italian or Irish surnames.

The USA fought and was on the winning side in two World Wars, from 1917-18, and 1941-45. It also fought the Korean War (1950-53), brought about by friction with the USSR, which ended in a truce. The Vietnam War (1965-75) ended less happily for the USA, which withdrew its troops due to pressure from home – unheard of before in wars, and largely due to television coverage of the war.

The USA since the 1920s

1927 US aviator Charles Lindberg became the first person to fly the Atlantic, solo.

1927 *The Jazz Singer*, the first "talkie" film, was released.

1929 The first Wall Street Crash. The stock market crashed, shares lost their value, in the panic hundreds of companies went bankrupt, businesses were ruined and millions of people lost their jobs.

1930 The Great Depression began. Millions of people were unemployed. To make matters worse, farmers of the Midwest plains were ruined when soil from their farms, exhausted by too much farming, blew away in dust storms.

1933-45 Franklin Delano Roosevelt was US president. He guided his country out of the Great Depression with social and economic measures called the "New Deal" and was commander-in-chief of US forces during World War 2. Roosevelt died in April 1945, a few days before German forces surrendered and the war in Europe ended.

1945 The USA dropped the first atomic bomb on Hiroshima, Japan (above right) and brought an end to World War 2.

1945 The USA became a founder member of the United Nations.

1953 Television invaded American living rooms.

1961 US Astronaut Alan Shepard became the first American in space.

1963 More than 200,000 civil rights demonstrators staged a march on Washington DC, for equality between all people, particularly between blacks and whites.

1969 US Astronaut Neil Armstrong became the first person on the Moon.

1973-74 The Watergate Affair revealed that government officials under US President Richard Nixon had lied, burgled, forged documents and tapped phone lines in order to discredit their political opponents. Nixon resigned.

1976 The USA celebrated its 200th year of independence.

1981 First successful test flight of the space shuttle programme. *Columbia* returned safely to Earth.

1986 Space shuttle *Challenger* exploded two minutes after blast off.

Dance marathons

The collapse of the Wall Street stock market in 1929 brought financial ruin to many people, and prompted a time of hardship in the USA which lasted almost a decade. Industry and agriculture went bankrupt. As a result many people went hungry, and many more lost their jobs and houses. One of the strangest ways to earn money was to enter a dance marathon. Couples danced in front of live audiences, with only brief rest periods, for days on end to win cash awards.

PHOTOS SOLD HERE MADE BY 'Rdm' Studio OPEN DAY & NIGHT.

We shall overcome...

Public protest became an acceptable way in the USA of seeking change during the turbulent 1960s. It was used by demonstrators against the Vietnam War and by civil rights leaders. Martin Luther King (shown here) was a brilliant leader whose inspiration and tireless work helped to call attention to the injustice of racial discrimination. He began his most famous speech with the words: "I have a dream..." He was awarded the Nobel Peace Prize in 1964, and was assassinated in 1968 in Memphis.

31

GOVERNMENT USA

Each of the 50 states of the USA has its own government, which is responsible for laws concerning local issues like highways, education and housing. The federal (national) government, in Washington DC, is headed by the president and is responsible for laws which affect all the people, such as civil rights and national security.

The American people vote for three types of officials: state politicians, state representatives in Washington, and for the president. Local representatives sent to Washington are called senators – who make up the Senate – and congressmen – who form the House of Representatives (see panel opposite). Each state sends two senators. The number of congressmen depends on the population of the state. It could be one for a small state, and up to 43 for a large state.

After the War of Independence the American people set up a document called the Constitution (1789). The Constitution sets out the basic rights of all citizens and the powers of state and federal governments.

Presidential elections

The president is a member of either the Democratic party or the Republican party. Presidential elections take place every four years. Delegates (candidates for the presidency) are elected by the people. Each party then chooses one delegate to stand for president. The winner of a national vote becomes the president. Much money is spent on promoting the delegates and film stars and other public figures give support to their chosen delegate. The election campaign below is taking place in South Carolina.

The White House
This enormous mansion in Washington is the official home and office of the President of the USA. It has 132 rooms.

Political parties
There are two main US political parties, the Republicans and the Democrats. The Republicans are conservative, and their symbol is an elephant. The Democrats are more liberal, and their symbol is a donkey. These animal mascots (above) began as political cartoons in the 1870s.

33

HEALTH, EDUCATION AND WELFARE

Although many people in the USA enjoy a high standard of living, some live in extreme poverty. There are poorly paid or unemployed people all over the country, but most are concentrated in the inner cities and in the southern states. In general, inner-city slums are caused by prosperous people moving to the suburbs. Poverty in the south is a result of the Civil War; the defeated south has never fully recovered its wealth.

The USA has no national health service, as there is in Britain. People must pay for medical care. Most of them join insurance schemes to meet the costs. Welfare and benefit schemes exist to help the poor, but they are inadequate to cope with the problems.

Education is free to all children in the USA. The quality of education varies, but on the whole is high. Almost one-half of all school-leavers, at age 18, continue with some form of further education at colleges and universities. These charge tuition fees. Scholarships (free places) are sometimes available to students who excel in studies or sports. Non-scholarship students sometimes go to class by day and work by night to earn their tuition fees.

US schools

Some Americans can stay in the education system from three to 26 years of age. Beginning with nursery school, the child progresses to kindergarten, elementary school (grades 1 to 6, at 6 to 11 years old), junior high school (grades 7 to 9, at 12 to 14 years old), and then high school (grades 10 to 12, 15 to 18 years old). The school day is much the same as in Europe, with lessons in languages, arts, science, religion and sports. These students are at a high school near New York. A high school diploma is needed for university or college.

The school bus

The bright yellow school bus takes students to and from elementary and high school. Surprisingly, the school bus became a political symbol when black underprivileged students were "bussed" to better-equipped schools. This highlighted the inequalities in education and living standards, which led to public protests.

Queuing for food

In many large American cities there are unemployed or low paid workers who cannot afford to feed and clothe themselves properly. Here, they queue for free food donated by a charity. This is in great contrast to the life style of the super-rich US billionaires, with their mansions, swimming pools and private planes.

35

EXCELLENCE IN THE ARTS

The USA has a fine tradition in the arts. One highly respected artist is Grandma Moses, who began painting at the age of 78 and continued past her 100th birthday. She painted scenes of country life in bright colours and in a very simple, almost child-like way called the "primitive" style. She won many awards and died in 1961, aged 101.

Another US painter is Grant Wood. He trained in Paris, then returned to the Midwest to portray scenes of everyday country life. His best-known painting is a group of local farmers called *American Gothic*.

America's best-known playwright is probably Arthur Miller, who was married to film star Marilyn Monroe during the 1950s. His bleak dramas such as *Death of a Salesman* (1949) show the difficulties of people's lives. Tennessee Williams wrote plays on similar themes, set in the southern states, such as *The Glass Menagerie*.

Admired US authors include Edgar Allen Poe (creator of the first detective story), John Steinbeck, Ernest Hemingway, and Herman Melville, who wrote the tale of the great white whale *Moby Dick*. The book *The Catcher in the Rye* (1951) by J D Salinger captured the public's imagination in the 1950s, with its story of the problems of teenage years and growing up.

"Two fathoms!"
Mark Twain wrote humorous stories such as *Tom Sawyer* (1875), an amusing and bitter-sweet tale of boyhood. His most famous book is probably *The Adventures of Huckleberry Finn* (1884), based on his experiences as a Mississippi steamboat pilot. Twain's real name was Samuel Clemens. He took his pen name from a river term meaning "two fathoms" – water deep enough for a riverboat to pass in safety.

Playwright Arthur Miller and his glamorous wife, film star Marilyn Monroe

The Wright buildings

Frank Lloyd Wright, the USA's foremost architect this century, designed startlingly original buildings, often using curves and block shapes, and usually made of concrete. Wright called his style "organic architecture", reflecting the shapes of nature. He designed New York's Guggenheim Museum building (begun in 1943), shown above.

A Warhol on the wall

Andy Warhol was one of the "pop artists" who made their name in the exciting decade of the 1960s. His simple idea of painting everyday items, such as a can of soup or a cola bottle, caught the public's imagination. Millions of people bought posters of his works to hang on their walls. Warhol also made experimental films and encouraged other artists. He died in 1987, aged 58.

ENTERTAINMENT USA

Popular culture is an important US export. American films and music are known across the world, with names such as the "all-American cowboy" actor John Wayne, singer Frank Sinatra, rock'n'roller Elvis Presley, actor Marlon Brando and rock musician Bruce "The Boss" Springsteen.

Hollywood, part of Los Angeles in California, is the heart of the film industry. In the 1930s and 1940s, film stars began to affect the way millions of people looked and dressed, and their movies offered escape from the problems of the Depression and war. The style and elegance of Hollywood's cinema heroes in the 1940s and 50s, such as Cary Grant and Katherine Hepburn, have given way to more recent "anti-heroes". These include Woody Allen, whose chaotic comedies reflect the confusion many Americans feel today. The films of actor-director Clint Eastwood, the "Man with no Name" in the cult Western *Fistful of Dollars*, have earned him more dollars than any other movie star.

C3PO and R2D2 – two of the robots from *Star Wars*

The success of *Star Wars*
During the 1960s, the domination of the Hollywood film studios was beginning to fade. Then Hollywood director George Lucas made *Star Wars*, in 1977. The *Star Wars* films have since become the biggest money-making series in cinema history, with their powerful combination of heroes, spaceships, aliens, robots and special effects.

Duck and Mouse
Donald Duck, along with his friends Pluto, Goofy and Mickey Mouse, were created by Walt Disney in the early 1930s. Disney was a pioneer of cartoon films, and later made movies with actors, such as Julie Andrews in *Mary Poppins* (1964). His *Snow White and the Seven Dwarfs* (1938) was the world's first full-length cartoon film.

Donald Duck

Minnie Mouse

Mickey Mouse

Singin' the blues

Blues music came originally from the southern USA. Its traditions were in the spiritual chants and working songs of slave gangs in the cotton fields. Their songs were often about sadness, hardship and "feelin' blue". In about 1910-20 the blues moved into city centres like New Orleans and Chicago, and brass instruments were added. A new form of music was invented, which became known as jazz. Here Edward "Duke" Ellington, a leading jazz composer and musician, plays for his friends during the 1930s.

The birth of rock 'n' roll

During the 1950s, young people decided they wanted their own music, different from the dance-band tunes liked by their parents. The USA's Country and Western music was blended with blues and beefed up to make the new, brash rock'n'roll rhythm. One of the most enduring rockers is Chuck Berry (right), who wrote hits such as *Johnny B Goode* (1958). Elvis Presley, a truck driver, burst onto the rock scene in the mid-1950s and went on to make a career as an actor and all-round singer (above). To millions of people Elvis was the "King", the greatest entertainer of the 1950s to 1970s. He died in 1977.

Chuck Berry

SPORT AND LEISURE

Sport is taken seriously in the USA, as a matter of individual achievement and national pride. Scholarships are offered to gifted athletes and sports people by colleges, and more money is spent on sport than on the entire coal and petroleum industries.

Baseball is one of the USA's national pastimes. Each autumn, when baseball's World Series is played, almost every American tunes in on radio or television. Each baseball team is based in a different city and is the source of much local pride.

Another US team game is American or "grid-iron" football. The players wear helmets and padded clothing to protect themselves during this very physical game. Talent scouts watch college games and recruit good new players into teams in the professional National Football League. This is divided into two "conferences", the National and American Conferences. Two top teams from each conference battle it out in the "Superbowl" each January.

The USA is a world leader in producing Olympic sports champions, particularly in events such as ice skating, swimming, track and field and ice hockey.

Leading the cheers
A mainstay at many big US sporting events are cheerleaders – girls dressed in team colours who wave pom-poms, twirl batons and dance in formation, urging the crowd to cheer for their team.

Baseball's Babe
George Herman "Babe" Ruth remains the US's best-known baseball player. During the 1920s his skill and flamboyant style enabled him to earn more money than the president. Ruth once said: "I had a better season than he did!".

Dribbling and shooting

Basketball is both a major sport and big business in the USA. Some of the players are more than 2 metres (6ft 8in) tall. The Harlem Globetrotters team (shown here) are the game's ambassadors, demonstrating their skills and entertaining crowds all over the world. Basketball is played in more schools and colleges than any other sport, and by girls as well as boys.

Jesse Owens

In the 1930s, James Cleveland "Jesse" Owens received 28 scholarship offers from various colleges because of his athletic skills. A championship sprinter and long jumper, he went on to win four gold medals in the 1936 Olympics in Berlin, Germany. His long jump record lasted 25 years.

FOOD, FAST . . . AND SLOW

Although the USA offers fine restaurants and excellent menus, both American and from other countries, it is perhaps better known for giving the world "fast food". Americans always seem to be in a hurry, and fast food fits in well with the way of life. It is cheap, quick to make and eat, and the idea can also be exported to increase business. In almost every major Western city there is now a McDonalds, Burger King or similar fast-food take-away restaurant. Other US fast food exports include hot dogs and Coca Cola.

"Pizza to go" is another American food idea. You order the pizza by telephone and it is delivered at your door, usually by a teenager in a van, then re-heated in your microwave oven.

American restaurants are clean and efficient, regardless of their style of food and the prices they charge. A glass of iced water is provided for each person, and food portions are generally large. Many restaurants provide "doggie bags" for leftover food to be taken home. Service is usually excellent, and staff love to tell their customers: "Have a Nice Day!"

Food from the world
America's cities, with many settlers from other countries, boast a huge range of ethnic foods. Italian and Chinese restaurants can be found in most towns. In New York "delis" (delicatessens) serve Jewish food such as salt beef. This restaurant window display is in the Chinese area (known as Chinatown) of New York.

Burgers to the world

During the 1950s fast food restaurants used to be called "drive-ins". You drove up in your car and parked, and food was delivered through the car window by a boy or girl called a "carhop". Drive-ins have largely given way to brightly-lit, family-style restaurants where the eating is done indoors. Foremost among these is McDonalds; the "drive-thru" one on the left is in North Windham, Maine, on the east coast.

Regional dishes

Various parts of the USA are known for their regional cooking. New England, in the north-east, specializes in seafood, especially lobster and clam chowder (clam shellfish made into a thick soup or stew). Southern states are known for their fried chicken and "grits", coarsely ground pieces of corn made into a paste, cooked and eaten instead of potatoes or pasta. Texas is known for huge outdoor barbecues, when an entire side of beef might be roasted on one spit. The south-west reflects its nearness to Mexico, specializing in tortillas (folded corn pancakes filled with meat, sauces and cheese) and spicy chilli sauces. Midwest menus advertise thick, succulent steaks and farm-fresh vegetables. California is known for healthy foods such as salads.

Clam chowder

Tortillas

Texan barbecue meal

Fried chicken and grits

43

TOMORROW'S USA

Compared to most countries, the standard of living in the USA is high. But increasingly, Americans are worried that prices are rising while natural resources diminish. The "Made in America" label is becoming rare as cheaper imported goods reach the shops. The gap between rich and poor is widening. Unemployment has increased, and the US crime rate is infamous as one of the worst in the Western world.

The average family is learning to cope with these changes. Many mothers now work to supplement the family income. Families are getting smaller, with only one or two children. The divorce rate is high and there are many one-parent families. There is increased awareness about saving natural resources: imported economy cars are commonplace, houses are better insulated, and the central heating temperatures are turned down, compared with 20 years ago.

Nuclear energy, once thought to be a solution to the energy crisis, is disliked by many people because of the risks of radioactive pollution. Public protests have led to cancellation of plans for new nuclear power stations. Some Americans are looking at other sources of energy, such as solar, wind and tidal power, for the 21st century.

President Ronald Reagan

Political interest

After the Watergate scandal of the 1970s, many Americans took more interest in politics. President Ronald Reagan, elected in 1981, has helped to improve relationships between the USA and USSR. But his officials were involved in the "Irangate" controversy in 1987, when armaments were sold to Iran and the money sent to Nicaragua to support the rebels there – all against US policy.

Jane Fonda, a US film star who has released many keep-fit books and videos

A cleaner, fitter America

People in the USA are becoming more aware of eating healthy food and keeping fit. Exercise in all forms is popular, from jogging to marathon-running to "working out" in the gymnasium. "Fast foods" are still consumed, but now have fewer additives and calories. In the 1930s, almost one-half of the adult US population smoked cigarettes. Today, it is only one-quarter.

Which channel?

Telecommunications continue to be a growth industry in the USA. Many American homes now have cable television, which allows a choice of up to 30 channels, 24 hours each day. Television has enormous influence, from advertising to holding debates between candidates in a presidential election.

Index

Acknowledgements
All illustrations by Ann Savage.
Photographic credits (a = above, b = below, m = middle, l = left, r = right):
Cover al GMBH Zefa, bl Chris Forsey, ar M Pitner/Zefa, br Chris Forsey;
page 8 Damm/Zefa; page 9 a cover, b Benser/Zefa: page 11 a Sclolz/Zefa,
b Steenmans/Zefa; page 12 BPCC/Aldus Archive; page 13 a Maney/Zefa,
b Heilman/Zefa; page 14 Macdonald/Aldus Archive; page 15 Koch/Zefa;
page 17 a Photri/Zefa, b Macdonald/Aldus Archive; page 19 a BPCC/
Aldus Archive, b Stockmarket/Zefa; page 20 cover; page 21 Steenmans/Zefa;
page 22 Macdonald/Aldus Archive; page 23 Maroon/Zefa; page 24 Zefa;
page 25 a and b BPCC/Aldus Archive; page 26, page 27 a and b, page 28,
page 31 Macdonald/Aldus Archive; page 32 Jim Bourg/Gamma-Liaison/
Frank Spooner Pictures; page 33 l Traver/Liaison/Frank Spooner Pictures,
r Connolly/Liaison/Frank Spooner Pictures; page 34 Bond/Zefa; page 35
BPCC/Aldus Archive; page 37 l The Bridgeman Art Library, r BBC Hulton
Picture Library; page 39 l and r Macdonald/Aldus Archive; page 40
Bettman Archive/Hulton Picture Library; page 41 Bob Thomas Sports
Photography; page 42 John Ross/Robert Harding Picture Library; page 43
Damm/Zefa; page 44 BBC Hulton Picture Library; page 45 a Benser/Zefa,
b Yvonne Hensey/Liaison/Gamma.